SCHOLASTIC

SMART Board® Lessons:
Capitalization & Punctuation

40 Ready-to-Use, Motivating Lessons on CD to Help You
Teach Essential Writing Skills

By Karen Kellaher and Diana Mai

D1410771

New York • Toronto • London • Auckland • Sydney
Mexico City • New Delhi • Hong Kong • Buenos Aires

Teaching *Resources*

To Abigail Rose   — D. M.

To Jeannie. I am so proud of you!   — K. K.

Both authors would like to thank
the Frelinghuysen Township School third-grade class of 2008–09.

Text © 2010 by Diana Mai and Karen M. Kellaher

Illustrated by Kelly J. Brownlee

Edited by Maria L. Chang and Betsy Henry Pringle

Designed by Rosanna Brockley

Design assistance by Richard Anderson, Tyler Freidenrich, and Shane Hartley

Cover design by Brian Larossa

Production by Jennifer Marx

SMART Board® Lessons: Capitalization & Punctuation is produced by **becker&mayer!**, Bellevue, WA 98004

Every effort has been made to trace copyright holders for the works reproduced in this book and CD, and the publishers apologize for any inadvertent omissions.

ISBN-13: 978-0-545-14025-6

ISBN-10: 0-545-14025-0

12168

Printed, manufactured, and assembled in Hong Kong, China 06/11.

4 5 6 7 8 9 10   16 15 14 13 12

Table of Contents

Introduction

Welcome to a whole new world in language arts education! By using the SMART Board to teach grammar and punctuation, you can turn a curriculum topic that's often dry and boring into one that's full of energy and interactivity. As we created the grammar lessons in this book and CD, we made several discoveries.

- The SMART Board offers instant lesson engagement. Whether you're teaching about nouns, narratives, or Roman numerals, you will have students' immediate attention. Many of today's kids are accustomed to games and gadgets that respond to the touch of a fingertip. A SMART Board grabs their attention in a way that blackboards and handouts fail to do.

- Because it offers a large, interactive display and opportunities for collaborative learning, the SMART Board is a smart way to teach students 21st-century skills like working in teams, marking text electronically, synthesizing information, organizing data, interpreting visual aids, and evaluating Web sites. These skills are an increasingly important part of the standards in many states.

- The SMART Board is easy to use, even for technophobes. Using the board itself and the accompanying Notebook software is fairly intuitive. On the interactive whiteboard, you can do anything you can do on your computer screen—and then some. So, even if you are just learning the technology, you can pull off a fun, effective lesson. The lessons on this CD will make it easy.

About the CD and Book

Make the most of SMART technology within your language arts curriculum. The SMART Notebook pages on the CD are a perfect way to teach grammar skills because they allow you to model concepts and skills for the whole class. You can read and analyze pieces of text together, deciding what words need to be capitalized and what pieces of punctuation are needed. You can move, highlight, underline, and change text right on the whiteboard. And, best of all, you can save *everything* for later use or review. Distribute copies of the completed Notebook pages for students to have on hand as rule reminders.

The CD contains five units on capitalization and punctuation skills. Each unit is on the CD as a Notebook file with eight interactive pages. These pages take advantage of the bells and whistles SMART technology has to offer without being overwhelming to the SMART Board novice. You'll find opportunities to use the Creative Pens, on-screen keyboard, graphic organizers, cloning tools, drag-and-drop feature, and more. Instructions for using each SMART tool are embedded in the lesson plans in this book.

Each unit on the CD introduces grammar skills in a gradual-release format. The first lesson in each unit introduces the topic, engages students' attention, and establishes what they already know. In the next six lessons, students collaboratively explore concrete skills related to the topic. In the last "lesson," students synthesize and apply what they have learned in a brief independent assignment. You may choose to have students complete this final Your Turn! activity in class or as a homework assignment.

In this book, you'll find easy-to-use lessons corresponding to each CD unit. Lessons include objectives, pacing suggestions, and step-by-step directions for teaching with each SMART Notebook page on the CD. They also correlate with important language arts standards.

Tech Tips

Although the SMART Capitalization and Punctuation CD was created using Notebook 10 software, you can use the activities with older versions of the software. If you are still getting the hang of your SMART Board, be sure to look for the technology tips offered at various points of use throughout the units. The following is an overview of the main Notebook features you will be using.

SMART Pens These are the black, red, green, and blue pens that came with your SMART Board. Use them to write directly on the screen in digital ink.

Creative Pens A student favorite, this tool allows you to draw fun lines made of smiley faces, stars, rainbow stripes, and more.

Magic Pen When students circle text or art with the Magic Pen, a spotlight focuses on the circled portion of the page. Everything else on the page goes dark temporarily. It's a dramatic way to focus attention on one element on a page!

Eraser Like its old-fashioned counterparts, this eraser removes unwanted writing. It will work on text and lines created with the SMART pens. It will not work on typed text or art objects.

On-Screen Keyboard If your students are adding text to a small field or simply prefer typing to writing freehand, use the on-screen keyboard. You can access it by touching the keyboard icon on the front tray of your SMART Board.

Properties Tool In several of the activities in this book, you'll be guided to use this feature to change the color or style of a SMART pen or to add color to a box.

Screen Shade A teacher favorite, this tool allows you to cover part of a page while focusing attention on another part. Activate the shade by clicking on the Screen Shade icon on your toolbar. Deactivate it by clicking again. To gradually open a shade that covers your screen, use one of the circular buttons on the shade itself to drag the shade open.

Correct Capitalization

Use these engaging Notebook pages to review capitalization basics and introduce more complicated areas of capitalization, such as capitalizing proper nouns and titles.

OBJECTIVES

Students will be able to:

- ✓ Understand the rules for capitalization.
- ✓ Recognize when a capital letter is missing from a word, proper noun, title, or sentence.
- ✓ Correctly insert capital letters in words, proper nouns, titles, and sentences.

TIME

About 3–4 class periods for Unit 1 (allow 15–20 minutes per lesson)

MEETING THE STANDARDS

This lesson correlates with the following writing standards for grades 3 through 6:

- • Students use Standard English conventions in all writing, such as sentence structure, grammar and usage, punctuation, capitalization, and spelling.
- • Students use capital letters correctly in sentences, for proper nouns, and in titles.

GETTING READY

Before students arrive, have your SMART Board ready to go. Load the Capitalization & Punctuation CD onto your host computer and copy the 1 SMART Capitalization Notebook file onto your hard drive. Open the local file. The first interactive page, *Calling All Capitals!* will appear on your SMART Board. If you wish, use your shade tool 🖳 to conceal the page until you are ready to begin.

Calling All Capitals!

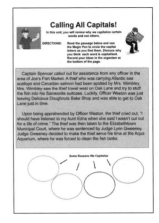

1. Display *Calling All Capitals!* on the SMART Board. To begin, ask students to think about where capital letters are used. They will likely respond with "the beginnings of sentences" and "the letter *I*." Discuss proper nouns if students do not come up with them on their own. Also, direct students to the title of the page, *Calling All Capitals!*, to discuss the use of capitals in titles.

2. Invite students to read the passage together with you. Then go back to the beginning and have students identify the capital letters in the passage. When each letter is identified, discuss with students the reason why the letter was capitalized. If students don't know the reason for a particular letter, explain briefly the rule concerning that letter and mention that you will learn more about the rule in subsequent lessons. Record students' observations about capitalization in the graphic organizer at the bottom of the page.

3. Discuss each correction with students to check for understanding.

TECH TIP

When the SMART Magic Pen is used to circle the capital letters, it will highlight only the letter in a lighted circle if an almost-perfect circle is drawn. If an imperfect circle is drawn with the Magic Pen, the circle will gradually disappear. Each of these functions is entertaining to students and places focus on the letter that is capitalized. Tell students that part of the fun in using the Magic Pen is that you never know what it will do!

Capitalization Doesn't Get a Vacation

1. Display *Capitalization Doesn't Get a Vacation* on the SMART Board. Point out that the first word of a sentence is always capitalized, as is the letter *I* when it is by itself as a pronoun. Explain that although this is a basic skill, more people are not following this grammar rule in the age of computers, e-mail, and texting. In the interest of speed, many people using e-mail and text messages neglect to capitalize the first word of a sentence or the letter *I*. Discuss the title, *Capitalization Doesn't Get a Vacation,* and why it is important to always capitalize the beginning of sentences and the letter *I*.

2. Discuss the proper editing mark (triple underline) used to show that a letter needs to be capitalized. Review the example given. If students do not already use the three underlines to show that a letter should be capitalized in regular practice, it may be helpful to show another example from the e-mail before having students attempt this on their own.

3. Read the first e-mail aloud together with students or ask one volunteer to read the e-mail. Then invite students to triple-underline each letter that needs to be capitalized and explain why they chose to underline the letter.

4. Repeat this process (step 3) for the second e-mail. Make sure to check for students' understanding and answer any questions.

5. Point out to students that although this lesson primarily focuses on the beginning of sentences and the letter *I*, it also previews capitalization rules that will be presented in subsequent lessons. Note: If students are not already familiar with proper nouns, you may wish to conduct a mini-lesson on them before proceeding to the next Notebook page.

TECH TIP

If students have trouble writing with the SMART pens, check that they are holding the stylus correctly. If a student's wrist or hand rubs against the board while writing, his or her writing will appear garbled and illegible. When using these pens, only the stylus tip should make contact with the SMART Board.

Take a Ride in the Capitalization Cab

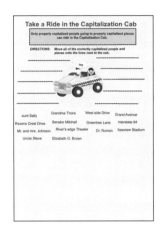

1. Display *Take a Ride in the Capitalization Cab* on the SMART Board. As you enter this Notebook page, have students pay attention to the board. The cab in the center of the page will spin and grab their attention.

2. Read the directions at the top of the page. Discuss which people and places should be capitalized. Explain that proper nouns are specific people, places, and things. For this activity, students must choose properly capitalized people and properly capitalized places.

3. Discuss that proper nouns must always be capitalized. Also, point out that proper nouns are often made up of more than one word. Explain that when a proper noun contains words such as *a, an, the,* and *of,* these words are not capitalized unless they are the first word of the proper noun.

4. Discuss that proper nouns include names showing a family relationship when used before a person's name or when directly addressing the person. They are not capitalized, however, when the familial descriptor follows a possessive pronoun.

> **Example:**　Grandma Rose is kind and sweet.
>
> I told Grandma that she was kind and sweet.
>
> *BUT*
>
> My grandmother is kind and sweet.

5. Draw students' attention back to the SMART Board. Scroll down the page to reveal the proper noun choices for students. Explain to students that they will simply touch a proper noun that is properly capitalized and drag it across the board onto the lines around the cab.

6. After students have moved all of the properly capitalized words onto the lines, draw their attention to the remaining words on the bottom of the board. To check for understanding, call on students to explain why those people or places were not allowed in the cab. See if they can determine how those people or places should have been capitalized.

TECH TIP

If students have trouble dragging the words across the board, demonstrate this process yourself. Sometimes it takes more than one try to get the word ready to move. Explain to students that they should not take their finger off the SMART Board once they have touched the word. The drag function works best when the student's finger stays in contact with the board.

Put Your Stamp on It

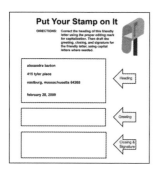

1. Display *Put Your Stamp on It* on the SMART Board. Ask students if they have ever written a letter to a friend. Did they notice all the words that had been capitalized?

2. Review the elements of a friendly letter. Make sure students are familiar with the heading, greeting, closing, and signature. If students have limited experience writing letters, it may be helpful to show an example of a friendly letter prior to viewing *Put Your Stamp on It*.

3. Discuss the heading and the proper nouns that are included in most headings (i.e., name, street, city, state, and month). Have students correct the name, address, and date in the heading. Remind them to use the editor's mark for capitalization (triple underline).

4. Scroll down to the greeting box on the page. Discuss to whom this friendly letter is written and how students would write out a greeting. Have a volunteer use a SMART pen to write out a simple greeting. Remind students that the words in the greeting must be capitalized and that the greeting of a friendly letter is followed by a comma.

5. Scroll down to the closing and signature box on the page. Discuss the components of a closing and signature for a friendly letter. Explain that only the first word of a closing is capitalized and that the closing is followed by a comma. Point out that the signature will always be capitalized because it's a name.

6. Discuss each correction to the heading as well as the text supplied by students in the greeting, closing, and signature to check for understanding.

Hey, We're Important, Too!

1. Display *Hey, We're Important, Too!* on the SMART Board. Explain to students that proper nouns include people, places, and things. When students think of proper nouns, they probably think mainly of people and places. This lesson explores some of the specific *things* that should be capitalized. Review each of these specific things with students.

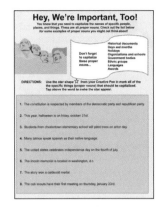

- Historical documents
- Days and months
- Holidays
- Organizations and schools

- Government bodies
- Ethnic groups
- Languages
- Awards

2. Read the directions together with students. Click on the SMART Creative Pen with your finger and choose the star shape. Demonstrate tapping your finger on the screen to make a single star appear.

3. Have students read each sentence aloud and look for words that should be capitalized. Once a word is chosen, have a student volunteer touch the SMART Board just above the letter that should be capitalized. The star shape will appear.

4. Call on other students to identify which type of specific thing needs to be capitalized. If necessary, direct students to the list of proper nouns at the top of the Notebook page to assist them.

5. To check for understanding, discuss why each word needed to be capitalized.

💡 **TECH TIP**

If a student needs to relocate a star that is already on the page, try one of these tricks:

- Switch tools! If the student tries to drag a star while the Creative Pen is still activated, he or she will end up putting a new star on the page every time he or she touches the board. Instead, switch back to the black arrow tool, then click on the star shape to move it. Once the star is placed to your satisfaction, re-select the star Creative Pen and continue with the activity.

- Alternatively, use the "Undo" button. Simply click on the back arrow to "undo" the last star you placed on the page. Put a new star exactly where you want it.

Yes, Sir!

1. Display *Yes, Sir!* on the SMART Board. Share with students that social and professional titles need to be capitalized. Many of these titles are familiar to students (Doctor, Judge, Mr., Mrs.). Other titles are not as familiar and may need to be explained, such as military titles (General, Colonel, and Lieutenant).

2. Explain to students that social and professional titles are capitalized only when they are directly in front of a person's name or when the person is being addressed directly. Review the example on *Yes, Sir!* to further demonstrate this rule.

> **Example:**   Mayor Smith is popular in our town.
>
> *BUT*
>
> The mayor was wearing a red shirt.

3. Read the directions aloud with students. Review the editing/proofreading marks for showing that a letter needs to be capitalized (triple underline) and for making a letter lowercase (slash through letter).

4. Read the sentences with students. Have a volunteer circle the sentence if it is correct or make corrections as needed using the editing marks. Discuss each correction with students to check for understanding. For best results, use the red, blue, or green pen to make your corrections stand out.

 TECH TIP

If circling or underline marks don't show up exactly where you want them, it's probably a sign that your SMART Board needs to be reoriented. Orienting ensures that your board is properly aligned. It is especially important to reorient if you are using a portable SMART Board unit. To orient, look on the Notebook software's startup menu.

Bookworms and Movie Buffs

1. Display *Bookworms and Movie Buffs* on the SMART Board. As you enter this Notebook page, have students pay close attention to the board. The movie reel will spin and grab their attention. Take this opportunity to ask students if they like books and movies. Have students share titles of some of their favorite books and movies.

2. Discuss that book and movie titles must be capitalized. Explain that titles of other works must be capitalized as well. Review the list of works on *Bookworms and Movie Buffs*.

   - Books
   - Newspapers
   - Magazines
   - Short stories
   - Poems
   - Plays
   - Movies
   - Songs

3. Explain that all important words in a title are capitalized, but not words such as *a, and, the, or,* and *of* unless it is the first or last word in the title. Read the directions on the page to introduce the specific rules.

4. Have students choose the words in the titles they think should be capitalized. Then invite them to highlight the letters that should be capitalized.

5. Check for understanding by discussing the reasons why students chose certain words to be capitalized over other words.

6. To extend learning, have students write out a list of their favorite books and movies using proper capitalization.

 TECH TIP ....

To highlight, have students click on the SMART pen and select the yellow highlighter from the right side of the pen toolbar. When the pen (or a finger) is tapped on the desired letter, a small circle of highlighter ink will illuminate the letter.

Capitalization: Your Turn!

1. Print and make copies of *Capitalization: Your Turn!* for students. Display the Notebook page on the SMART Board. Explain that students will complete this page on their own, either in class or for homework, to apply what they have learned about the rules of capitalization.

2. Review the directions with students, explaining that they will use proper editing marks to correct the capitalization errors in each sentence. Then they will rewrite the sentences correctly on the line provided. Distribute copies of the worksheet.

3. Review the exercise individually or as a class to assess student learning of capitalization concepts.

Sentence Stoppers

Just as red lights and road signs control the flow of traffic, appropriate ending punctuation helps readers navigate a piece of text. Use these Notebook pages and lessons to help developing writers understand when and how to bring each sentence to a happy ending.

OBJECTIVES

Students will be able to:

✓ Understand the purpose of ending punctuation.

✓ Recognize when to use a period, question mark, or exclamation point.

✓ Edit sentences for appropriate ending punctuation.

✓ Use ending punctuation to turn run-ons into sentences.

TIME

About 3–4 class periods for Unit 2 (allow 15–20 minutes per lesson)

MEETING THE STANDARDS

This lesson correlates with the following writing standards for grades 3 through 6:

• Students use Standard English conventions in all writing, such as sentence structure, grammar and usage, punctuation, capitalization, and spelling.

• Students correctly use periods, question marks, and exclamation points.

GETTING READY

Before students arrive, have your SMART Board ready to go. Load the Capitalization & Punctuation CD onto your host computer and copy the 2 SMART Sentence Stoppers Notebook file onto your hard drive. Open the local file. The first interactive page, *Sentence Stoppers*, will appear on your SMART Board. If you wish, use your Screen Shade tool to conceal the page until you are ready to begin.

Sentence Stoppers

1. To begin, have students recall the different forms of punctuation that can be used to end a sentence. Review what students already know about when to use periods, question marks, and exclamation points. Explain that this unit will review the basics of ending punctuation and help students apply the rules to their own writing.

2. Display *Sentence Stoppers* on the SMART Board and read the directions on the page. Explain that you are going to read the passage aloud. Challenge students to pay close attention to how the text sounds without ending punctuation. As you read, exaggerate the effect that lack of punctuation has on fluency: Do not pause between sentences. Be careful not to automatically change your inflection or intonation for sentences that seem to be questions or exclamations. (For this read-aloud, it is recommended that you do the reading yourself rather than ask for a student volunteer.)

3. When you finish reading, ask students what they noticed about the effects of the lack of punctuation. Using the on-screen keyboard or the SMART pens, record their observations on the left side of the "What We Notice" chart at the bottom of the page. Observations might include:

    -   Ideas were all jumbled together.

    -   You couldn't tell which ideas were important.

    -   It was hard to make sense of the story.

4. Invite a student volunteer to approach the SMART Board and rub the SMART eraser over the story. Appropriate ending punctuation will be revealed. Read the story once again, this time emphasizing how the sentence-ending punctuation boosts fluency. Pause between sentences, read exclamations and commands with urgency and excitement, and use an upward inflection for questions.

5. Again, ask students what they noticed when punctuation was added and record their observations on the chart. Observations might include:

    -   You could hear each idea.

    -   Questions sounded different from statements.

    -   There was more excitement and feeling in the story.

    -   It was easier to make sense of the story.

Graph It!

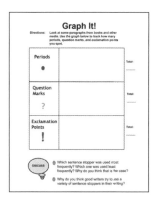

1. In this lesson, students will examine real fiction and nonfiction texts and make two important observations. One is that good writers use a variety of sentence types (statements, exclamations, and questions) to make their writing sound lively and interesting. The second is that statement sentences (ending in periods) are by far the most frequently used. To prepare, have on hand a variety of texts for students to choose from: textbooks, fiction and nonfiction trade books, magazines, newspapers, and so on.

2. Divide students into pairs or small groups and have each team select a text. Display *Graph It!* on the SMART Board and read the directions for the page. Direct each group to randomly select a three-paragraph section of the text they have chosen. Have team members collaborate to count and tally the number of periods, question marks, and exclamation points in their three paragraphs.

3. Allow several minutes for teams to complete the activity. Then redirect students' attention to the SMART Board. Explain that the class is going to compile all of the teams' findings by creating a pictograph. Begin by asking each group to report the number of periods it found. As a group shares its number, demonstrate adding a matching number of periods to the graph. The graph has been set up so that you can "infinitely clone" the purple period in the column on the left. In SMART Board lingo, that means it will make a new copy each time you touch it. Simply click on or touch the period and drag it to the graph space on the right. Repeat as many times as necessary.

4. Continue by having each group report the number of question marks and exclamation points they have found. Fill in the corresponding spaces on the graph with the correct number of punctuation marks. (Remember, click on or touch and drag the question mark or exclamation point to clone it.)

5. Have students count the number of each sentence stopper they found. Use the SMART pen to record each total on the line to the right of the graph.

6. Wrap up by discussing sentence variety, using the prompts at the bottom of the Notebook page. Remind students that, like the models they studied, their own reports and stories should use mostly statements ending in periods. They should use occasional questions and exclamations to add spice and variety.

Using Periods

1. Tap into prior knowledge by asking students to name two kinds of sentences that end in periods. Many students will immediately think of *declarative sentences,* or statements. Elicit a few examples of declarative sentences. If students have trouble thinking of a second type of sentence that ends in a period, offer clues by giving students gentle commands, such as the following: *Think carefully. Use your head. Give an example.* Guide students to understand that the second type of sentence that calls for a period is a command, also known as an *imperative sentence.*

2. Display *Using Periods* on the SMART Board and read the examples and directions together. Point out that the left side of the ladybug is for declarative sentences, while the right side is for imperative sentences. Invite a student volunteer to read aloud one sentence. Have him or her drag and drop the sentence "dot" onto the correct side of the ladybug and explain his or her thinking. (If students have never used this feature of the SMART Board before, demonstrate how easy it is to place a finger on the shape and move it across the page.)

3. Repeat, inviting additional volunteers to read and move the remaining sentences.

4. For the two blank dots at the bottom of each half, have students generate sample sentences of their own. Encourage students to give you one declarative and one imperative sentence. Use the on-screen keyboard to type a sentence into each dot. To activate the on-screen keyboard, touch the keyboard icon on your SMART pen tray. Use the keyboard that appears to begin typing. When you finish typing, move your text into the ladybug dot. First, slide the small circles on either side of your text box in to make your text box small enough to fit inside the dot. Then drag the text box to the correct ladybug dot.

5. If you wish, extend the lesson by spending a few minutes exploring imperative sentences at greater length. Explain that the subject of an imperative sentence is the pronoun *you,* even though the word does not appear in the sentence:

> **Example:** (You) Make the bed.
>
> (You) Turn the page now.

Point out that not all imperative sentences end in a period. Highlight the word *gentle* at the top of the Notebook page and explain that periods are used to end imperatives that are not urgent. If a command is shouted or spoken urgently, the sentence ends in an exclamation point instead.

> **Example:** Turn on channel 12, please.
>
> *BUT*
>
> Turn that TV down right now!

TECH TIP

When you are using the on-screen keyboard, touch the blue "up" arrow to make the next character you type a capital.

Question Mark Clues

1. Display *Question Mark Clues* on the SMART Board and read Rule 1 at the top of the page. Explain to students that a question is an *interrogative sentence*.

2. Model how to use your finger as a highlighter. To access the highlighter, use your finger to click on the SMART pen tool. Select the thick yellow highlighter. Think aloud as you begin reading the words in the box:

   The word when *is a question word. I use it to ask things like, "When does class begin?" I will highlight* when *to show that it can be used to start a question. Who can find another question word in the box?*

3. Invite student volunteers to find examples of question starters in the box and highlight them with a finger. Keep in mind that once the highlighter is activated, students do not need to keep going back to the toolbar to select it. To deactivate the highlighter, just click on the black arrow on your toolbar.

4. Ask student volunteers to use the SMART pen to write one or two questions that begin with question words from the box.

5. Introduce the second half of the activity by reading Rule 2 and pointing out that not all questions begin with question words. Another way to write or ask a question is to add a question tag to the end of a declarative sentence. Read aloud the example and have students follow the example's model to complete the two additional examples.

 **TECH TIP**

When using the SMART Board with younger students, make the toolbar more accessible by placing it at the bottom of your screen. Click the up-and-down arrow on the right side of the toolbar to move it up or down.

Too Much Excitement!

1. Share the title of this activity with your class and explain that the title hints at one of the most common punctuation mistakes student writers make. Challenge students to guess what that mistake might be. *(Overusing exclamation points)* Display *Too Much Excitement!* on the SMART Board and read the directions and examples at the top of the page. Discuss briefly why peppering a story or report with exclamation points is not effective: It reduces the impact of any exclamation points that are truly necessary. It is jarring to the reader and suggests that the writer can't decide what is important or surprising.

2. Explain that as students read the story on this page, they will remove some of the exclamation points. Point out that there is no one "right" way to do the activity. Some students may feel that a particular exclamation point is helpful, while others may feel it is unnecessary. However, explain there is no doubt that this passage has entirely too many.

3. Have students read the first paragraph of the story aloud from their seats. Ask a student volunteer to identify an exclamation point that he or she thinks is out of place and then approach the SMART Board. Have the student drag the unnecessary exclamation point to the trash at the side of the Notebook page. Then, have him or her use the red SMART pen to add a period to the end of the sentence in the story.

4. Repeat, inviting other volunteers to point out, remove, and replace other extraneous exclamation points. If students begin to remove all of the exclamation points from the story, encourage them to leave one or two in the story, and challenge them to identify which ones they think are most necessary.

5. Have students discuss types of writing that might include more exclamations than usual (dialogue, action stories, etc.) and other forms of writing that may not use any exclamations at all (instruction manuals, news reports).

Stop That Sentence!

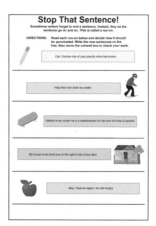

1. Point out that another common mistake writers make is to forget ending punctuation and allow several ideas to run together. Ask students if anyone knows the name for this kind of mistake. *(A run-on)*

2. Display *Stop That Sentence!* on the SMART Board and read the directions together. Have students read the text in the yellow box and tell how many sentences the text actually contains. *(Two)* Allow a minute or two for students to rewrite the sentences in their notebooks or on scrap paper, using correct punctuation and capitalization.

3. Have students describe how they changed the text to correctly punctuate and capitalize those sentences. Using the SMART pen, follow students' instructions and rewrite the two revised sentences on the line.

4. If students are satisfied with the way the sentences are punctuated and capitalized, move the yellow box aside to reveal the correctly punctuated "answer."

5. Have students take several minutes to rewrite the sentences in the remaining boxes. Then, invite volunteers to rewrite the text on the SMART Board. After each volunteer finishes, ask the class if they agree or would make any changes. Move aside the box to check the work.

 TECH TIP

For this activity, it is important to rewrite the sentences rather than use editing marks. If you add editing marks to the colored boxes, the marks will stay behind when you move the boxes aside.

Obey the Signs

1. Display *Obey the Signs* on the SMART Board. Explain that this page reviews what students have learned about sentence-ending punctuation. Read the directions and remind students how to move a text block by dragging it across a Notebook page. Demonstrate with the first sentence on the page:

   "What are your plans for Saturday" sounds like a question to me, so I am going to move this sentence down to the question mark box on the organizer.

2. Have students take turns reading the sentences aloud and placing them into the correct part of the punctuation graphic organizer.

3. After you finish placing the sentences, direct students' attention to the discussion prompt at the bottom of the screen. Have students use the smiley face Creative Pen to put a smiley face next to any sentence that could be punctuated in two different ways. Guide students to understand that, in some cases, the punctuation of a sentence depends on the tone or level of urgency the writer wishes to convey. Discuss the examples below with students.

Example:	Help me! I've been bitten by a snake.
	BUT
	Help me. I just don't understand this math problem.
	Get down, Kate! You're going to fall!
	BUT
	Get down, Kate. It's someone else's turn on the swings.

 **TECH TIP**

Use your finger as the pen by going to Creative Pens on your toolbar and selecting the smiley face style. Then tap your finger on the screen one time to make a single smiley face appear.

Sentence Stoppers: Your Turn!

1. Print and make copies of *Sentence Stoppers: Your Turn!* for students. Display the Notebook page on the SMART Board. Explain that students will complete this page on their own, either in class or for homework, to apply what they have learned about the uses of periods, exclamation points, and question marks.

2. Review the directions with students, explaining that they will add ending punctuation to the sentences using proper editing marks. Distribute copies of the worksheet.

3. Review the exercise individually or as a whole class to check for understanding.

Commas in Place

Some students pepper every sentence with commas. Others forget to use them entirely! Cement the rules and provide plenty of practice with the comma activities in this unit.

OBJECTIVES

Students will be able to:

- ✓ Use commas to separate items in a series.

- ✓ Use commas when writing dates and place names.

- ✓ Use commas when needed with quotation marks.

- ✓ Use commas to separate clauses from the rest of a sentence, when appropriate.

- ✓ Edit text for comma usage.

TIME

About 3–4 class periods for Unit 3 (allow 15–20 minutes per lesson)

MEETING THE STANDARDS

This lesson correlates with the following writing standard for grades 3 through 6:

- • Students apply punctuation conventions correctly in writing, including commas.

GETTING READY

Before students arrive, have your SMART Board ready to go. Load the Capitalization & Punctuation CD onto your host computer and copy the 3 SMART Commas Notebook file onto your hard drive. Open the local file. The first interactive page, *Commas at Work*, will appear on your SMART Board. If you wish, use your Screen Shade tool to conceal the page until you are ready to begin.

Commas at Work

1. Display *Commas at Work* on the SMART Board and read the page directions aloud. To illustrate the concept that commas tell readers to pause, share the following sentence with students. First, read the sentence normally, pausing briefly at each comma. Then read it without pausing at the commas. Discuss how the commas aid in comprehension.

   I invited John, Paul, Hillary, and Kay.

2. Have students read the first prompt and try to unscramble the letters to complete the comma rule. Invite a volunteer to move the letters around to form the word *list*. Invite a second volunteer to move aside the picture of the comma to reveal an example of a sentence that illustrates the rule. Have students brainstorm another sentence that uses commas in this fashion.

3. Have students unscramble the remaining comma rules. For each rule, move the comma picture to reveal an example. The remaining rules are:

   - Use a comma when you write a DATE.

   - Use a comma to separate a CITY from a STATE.

   - Use a comma to separate a direct QUOTATION from the rest of the sentence.

   - Use a comma to separate clauses, or parts of a SENTENCE.

   - Use commas to punctuate the greeting and closing of a friendly LETTER.

4. Explain that students are going to explore each of these rules in greater detail in this unit.

 TECH TIP

If students are just getting to know the SMART Board, demonstrate using your finger to "click" on a letter and move it around. Explain to students that their finger is serving as a computer mouse.

Check Your List!

1. Display *Check Your List!* on the SMART Board. Have students recall the first comma rule they read in the previous activity—using commas to separate items in a list or series. Guide students to understand that while we usually think of a list as a series of nouns (as in a shopping list), we can also list verbs or other parts of speech. Share the examples in the colored boxes to illustrate.

2. Read the activity directions together. Then read aloud the first sentence in the news story and discuss whether a comma is needed to separate items in a series. (*No, because there is no series.*) Repeat with the second sentence. Elicit that the verbs *research*, *write*, and *practice* should be separated by commas.

3. Demonstrate using a finger to drag the red comma from the box to the sentence. Drop the comma just after the word *research*. Then invite a student volunteer to drag another comma to the space just after the word *write*. Notice that the comma shape has been "infinitely cloned" so it will make a new copy each time you touch it.

4. Continue reading the news story as a class, inviting students to place commas where needed. When you finish, count the commas you have used. Remind students that the directions instructed them to use 12 commas. If you have used fewer than or more than 12, reread the story to check for comma mistakes.

💡 TECH TIP

Did you copy too many commas? To delete one (or any unwanted object on a Notebook page), select it by clicking on it with your finger. Check that a blue dotted line surrounds the selected object. Then touch the red X in your toolbar.

A Time and a Place

1. Explain to students that one common reason we use commas is to separate a date and year. Write today's date on the top of the Notebook page and ask students to think about why the comma is helpful to readers. *(It avoids confusion, since the date and year are both numbers.)*

2. Review that another everyday way we use commas is to write place names. We use a comma to separate a city name from a state or country name. Have students cite some examples.

3. Display *A Time and a Place* on the SMART Board and read the page introduction. Read and discuss the examples together, making sure students understand that if a sentence continues after a date or place name, a second comma must be used after the date or place name. Give some additional examples, and challenge students to work in pairs to brainstorm examples of their own.

4. Read sentence number 1 and ask students to identify any spots where a comma is needed. Then invite a volunteer to approach the SMART Board. Explain that you are going to check whether the class was right by having the volunteer rub the SMART eraser over the sentence. As he or she does so, commas will be revealed in their correct positions. Discuss whether students were correct.

5. Read the remaining sentences. Discuss where commas belong, then have students erase over each sentence to check. Pay special attention to sentences 6, 7, and 8. In these sentences, a second comma is needed because the date or place name appears in the middle of the sentence.

6. Tell students that one of the sentences on the Notebook page spotlights a use for commas that you have not yet discussed. Challenge students to find the additional example of comma usage. *(Sentence 8 shows that a comma is used to separate digits in the number 800,000.)*

7. If you wish, print out the page with the commas in position and make a copy for each student.

TECH TIP

When using your SMART eraser for an activity like this one, remind students to rub the eraser over only the sentence being discussed. Erasing over other sentences will reveal the punctuation prematurely.

Can I Quote You?

1. Prepare for the activity by having on hand a variety of texts for students to peruse. Chapter books, newspapers, and magazines that contain quotations are perfect for this purpose.

2. Display *Can I Quote You?* on the SMART Board. Read aloud the page introduction and the three rules that apply to using commas with quotations. Guide students to understand that a comma is usually needed to separate a direct quote from a speech tag (the phrase that identifies the speaker). An exception is when the direct quote ends in a question mark or exclamation point and comes before the speech tag, as in the following examples.

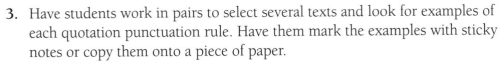

> **Example:** "Stop right there!" shouted the policeman.
>
> "Are you ready for lunch?" she asked.

3. Have students work in pairs to select several texts and look for examples of each quotation punctuation rule. Have them mark the examples with sticky notes or copy them onto a piece of paper.

4. Invite pairs to share the examples they found. Record one example of each rule in the organizer at the top of the Notebook page.

5. Scroll down to the second part of the page. Explain that in this portion of the page, students will identify the speech tag in each sentence and add a comma to separate the speech tag from the quotation, if one is needed. Have volunteers use the SMART pens to mark each sentence.

6. As students add commas to the sample sentences, emphasize that the comma belongs inside the quotation marks when the quotation precedes the speech tag. When you discuss sentence 4, check that students understand why no comma is needed. (*The quotation ends in an exclamation point.*)

7. Save your class's work and make a copy for each student.

Sentence Glue

1. Read aloud several compound sentences like the ones below and ask students what they notice about the sentences. Guide students to notice that each of the sentences is made up of two smaller complete sentences joined by a word like *and* or *but*. Explain that this type of sentence is called a *compound sentence* and that the connecting word is known as a *conjunction*. Explain that a comma helps the conjunction join the two small sentences together.

> **Example:** The wind blew, and the door slammed open.
>
> We ran out of milk, but I can go to the store to buy some.

2. Display *Sentence Glue* on the SMART Board and read the introduction and directions for the page. If necessary, review the definitions of subject and predicate to help students recognize a complete sentence. For the purposes of this activity, focus on simple subjects and predicates.

> • A *simple subject* is the noun that tells whom or what a sentence is about.
>
> • A *simple predicate* is the verb that tells what the subject is or does.

3. Invite a student volunteer to approach the SMART Board and read aloud the first sentence in column A. Ask him or her to choose the sentence in column B that connects to the first sentence in a way that makes sense. Have the student use a Creative Pen to draw a line from the sentence in column A to the sentence in column B.

4. Have the student use a regular SMART pen to write the newly created compound sentence on the line. Remind the student to connect the two sentence parts with a comma followed by *and* or *but*. Encourage the student to share his or her thinking about which coordinating conjunction makes sense in the sentence, and why.

5. Repeat steps 3 and 4 with the remaining sentences in columns A and B until all four lines are filled.

6. Explain to students that *and* and *but* are not the only words that can be used to combine smaller sentences. A complete list of coordinating conjunctions is cited at left. If you wish, offer the mnemonic FANBOYS to help students remember these words. Remind students that whenever these words are used to link two complete sentences, a comma is needed.

7. Extend the lesson by having students write original compound sentences that use a comma followed by a coordinating conjunction.

Coordinating Conjunctions

for	but
and	or
nor	yet
	so

Just Because

1. Display *Just Because* on the SMART Board. Explain that, like the previous activity, this page instructs students on using commas to join sentence parts together. In this case, students will learn when to use commas with adverb clauses.

2. Explain to younger students that an *adverb clause* begins with a word like *while*, *because*, *if*, or *when*. The clause can go at the beginning or ending of the sentence. It helps answer a question like, *When did the action happen?* or *Why did the action happen?*

3. You might wish to go into greater detail with older students. Explain that an adverb clause is not a complete sentence. It modifies the verb in the main clause (the sentence) to which the adverb clause is attached. It tells how, when, why, how much, to what extent, or under what conditions the action in the main clause takes place.

4. Discuss the comma rules at the top of the page. Note that if an adverb clause comes at the beginning of a sentence, a comma is needed. If it comes at the end of the sentence, no comma is needed.

5. Invite a student volunteer to choose an adverb clause from column A and find a corresponding sentence from column B. Have the student "drag and drop" both sentence parts into the first box. Have the student follow the directions in the box to create a sentence in which the adverb clause appears at the beginning. Remind the student to use a SMART pen to add a comma after the adverb clause and ending punctuation after the last word in the sentence.

6. Repeat step 5. Have another volunteer choose a new adverb clause and create a second sentence in which the adverb clause comes at the beginning.

7. Once both green boxes are full, explain that students are going to create some sentences in which the adverb clause comes at the end. Have a volunteer drag and drop an adverb clause and sentence into the red box and follow the directions. Remind students that no comma is needed when an adverb clause appears at the end of the sentence.

8. Repeat step 7. To fill the final red box, have a volunteer drag and drop items to create a second sentence in which the adverb clause comes at the end of the sentence.

Extra! Extra!

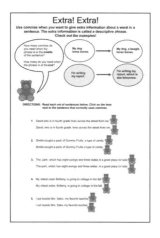

1. Tell students they will learn one more rule for using commas. Display *Extra! Extra!* on the SMART Board and read the introduction and examples together. Use the SMART highlighter (find this under SMART pens in the toolbar) to highlight the descriptive phrase in each example.

2. Call students' attention to the prompt in the speech bubble. How many commas are needed if the descriptive phrase is at the end of the sentence? (*One*) How many commas are needed if the descriptive phrase appears in the middle of the sentence? (*Two*) Remind students that they followed a similar rule when using commas to punctuate dates and place names.

3. To check for understanding, have students generate additional examples of sentences with descriptive phrases. Or, offer a simple sentence and challenge students to add a descriptive phrase.

> **Example:**   Our classroom is at the end of the hall.
>
> Our classroom, a bright and sunny space, is at the end of the hall.

4. Have students begin the activity by reading aloud the first sentence. Instruct them to identify the descriptive phrase in the sentence and to look carefully at both versions of the sentence. Ask students to tell which sentence uses commas correctly to punctuate the descriptive phrase.

5. When students agree, invite a volunteer to touch the picture at the end of the sentence. If the sentence is punctuated correctly, the picture will spin. If the sentence is not punctuated correctly, nothing will happen. Discuss with students why the other sentence choice was incorrect. (*In sentence 1, the incorrect choice does not use commas to set off the descriptive phrase.*)

6. Have students continue with sentences 2 through 5, clicking on the pictures to check their work. In each instance, discuss why each correct choice is properly punctuated.

Commas: Your Turn!

1. Print and make copies of *Commas: Your Turn!* for students. Display the Notebook page on the SMART Board. Explain that students will complete this page on their own, either in class or for homework, to apply what they have learned about comma usage.

2. Review the directions with students, explaining they will use the editing symbol in the box to add commas to the friendly letter on the page. If students are unfamiliar with the editing symbol, take a moment to demonstrate. Use the red SMART pen to add the first comma to the exercise (add a comma between Oak View and PA in the return address). Explain that you are using red so your editing marks will stand out, and encourage students to do the same. Distribute copies of the worksheet.

3. If you are working with younger or struggling students, consider differentiating the activity by alerting students that there are a total of 17 missing commas.

Quotation Marks Speak

Quotation marks are used to set apart dialogue and the titles of certain artistic works. This SMART unit is designed to be engaging and fun, and it will help introduce as well as reinforce the proper use of quotation marks.

OBJECTIVES

Students will be able to:

✓ Understand the conventions for using quotation marks in American English.

✓ Recognize when someone is speaking in a sentence and properly punctuate with quotation marks.

✓ Identify and write dialogue using proper punctuation.

✓ Use quotation marks to identify the names of artistic works.

TIME

About 3–4 class periods for Unit 4 (allow 15–20 minutes per lesson)

MEETING THE STANDARDS

This lesson correlates with the following writing standards for grades 3 through 6:

• Students use Standard English conventions in all writing, such as sentence structure, grammar and usage, punctuation, capitalization, and spelling.

• Students use punctuation correctly in sentences, such as ending punctuation, commas, and quotation marks in dialogue.

GETTING READY

Before students arrive, have your SMART Board ready to go. Load the Capitalization & Punctuation CD onto your host computer and copy the 4 SMART Quotation Marks Notebook file onto your hard drive. Open the local file. The first interactive page, *Missing Marks*, will appear on your SMART Board. If you wish, use your Screen Shade tool to conceal the page until you are ready to begin.

Missing Marks

1. To begin, ask students to think about where they have seen quotation marks before. They will likely respond by saying they have seen them in fiction stories. If not, show students a sample picture book (with larger type) to remind them of quotation marks in dialogue. Some students may already use quotation marks in their own writing. If so, discuss where they think quotation marks should be used in writing.

2. Display *Missing Marks* on the SMART Board and read the introduction and activity directions together with students. Review that both sets of quotation marks typically curve toward the quoted material to enclose it.

3. Emphasize that quotation marks should "hug," or surround, the quoted words and any punctuation that goes with those words (commas, periods, and so on). One way to illustrate this point with younger students or kinesthetic learners is to have four student volunteers act out a piece of dialogue. Have one student put her arms out in the shape of quotation marks (arms outstretched, one higher than the other), one student act as the words being spoken (put hands by mouth and pretend to be speaking with hands), one student crouched down as a period or standing tall as an exclamation mark, and a final student putting her arms out in the shape of quotation marks but on the opposite side as the first volunteer.

4. Read the first sentence together. Explain that some of the quotation marks are already in the sentence and that students need to fill in the other part of each set. Students will use a SMART pen to write in the missing quotation marks. If you would like to use a purple pen to match the purple quotes already in place, simply pick up the regular black SMART pen and use it to click on the Tool Properties box. Choose Line Style. Then choose the purple color. Your black pen will temporarily write with purple ink.

5. After adding the missing quotation marks, students can check their work by rubbing the SMART eraser on the blank box below the corrected sentence. The correctly punctuated sentence will be revealed.

💡 TECH TIP

If you choose to change a pen color, remember that the pen will revert to its original color once you place it back in its tray. Have students refrain from putting the pen back in the SMART Board tray until you have completed the page.

That's Exactly It!

1. Display *That's Exactly It!* on the SMART Board. Discuss with students that quotation marks are used to enclose a speaker's exact words. Point out that the speech tag (the part of the sentence that identifies the speaker) should not be inside the quotation marks. Explain that the name of the speaker and verbs such as *said, asked, replied,* and *responded* are part of the speech tag and should be outside of the quotation marks.

2. Read the directions and examples with students. Discuss the difference between quoting and paraphrasing a person's words. If you wish, demonstrate the difference by asking a student to tell you what he or she had for breakfast. Give an example of a direct quote and a paraphrased statement.

> **Example:** **Quote:** Stella said, "I had oatmeal and half a piece of toast."
>
> **Paraphrase:** Stella said she had eaten oatmeal and some toast for breakfast.

3. Explain that in this activity students will decide if each statement is a direct quote or a paraphrased statement. If it is a quote, students will clone the quotation mark in the speech bubble and drag it to the proper spots in the sentence. If you have not yet used the clone function with your class, you may need to model this process. To simplify the activity, the quotation mark has been set up using the "infinite cloner" tool. To clone the mark, simply touch it and drag.

4. Remind students to write a *P* after each sentence that paraphrases words instead of quoting them.

5. Discuss each sentence with students to check for understanding.

6. To extend the lesson, have students look for examples of direct quotations and paraphrased statements in newspaper or magazine articles.

💡 TECH TIP

If students have trouble dragging the quotation marks across the SMART Board, demonstrate this process yourself. Explain that students should not take their finger off the SMART Board once they have touched a word. The drag function won't work if the student's finger breaks contact with the board.

Let's Talk!

1. Display *Let's Talk!* on the SMART Board. Initiate a discussion about dialogue. Ask students where they have seen dialogue (fiction books, for example) and where they may have used dialogue (writing stories). Discuss the importance of designating a speaker when writing dialogue. Ask students what would happen if the speaker was not identified in dialogue. Students will probably respond by saying that you would not know who was talking and that it would be a confusing story.

2. Read the directions on *Let's Talk!* together with students. Discuss that students will write dialogue, or conversation, for three different scenarios. Emphasize that the student-created dialogue should be brief—one quotation per character is sufficient.

3. Have students read the first scenario aloud. Call on volunteers to share what Marty and his father might be saying to one another. Using the SMART pen or the on-screen keyboard, enter the dialogue into the white box. If you have younger students, you may find it easiest to write or type the text yourself. If you have older students, have them work directly on the SMART Board. In either case, remind students to use quotation marks and other appropriate punctuation and to identify each speaker.

TECH TIP

When typing text onto a SMART Notebook page, use a clear and simple font such as Arial. Fancier fonts may look great on a regular computer screen, but they are not always legible on the bigger SMART Board screen.

4. If students struggle with creating their own dialogue (or if you would like to modify ahead of time to differentiate instruction), write your own dialogue in the boxes and have students add speech tags to identify the speaker. If you wish, write or type the following dialogue, leaving out the underlined portions. Have students add their own speech tags.

> **For picture 1:**
>
> "Can I help?" <u>asked Marty.</u>
>
> "Sure, you can hold the pump while I get the tire ready," <u>Dad replied.</u>
>
> **For picture 2:**
>
> "I'll buy the invitations," <u>Maggie said.</u>
>
> "And I'll buy the balloons and cake," <u>her sister offered.</u>
>
> **For picture 3:**
>
> "I'll do the animal report," <u>Maria offered.</u>
>
> "I can make the poster," <u>Jonah volunteered.</u>
>
> "I can make a model of our animal," <u>Kayla chimed in.</u>

5. Discuss students' work.

Separating Speakers

1. Display *Separating Speakers* on the SMART Board. Activate prior knowledge by asking students when writers should start a new paragraph. They will probably respond that writers should begin a new paragraph each time they start talking about a new idea.

2. Explain that the "new idea" rule applies to quotations, too. Whenever a writer is drafting a conversation, he or she should start a new paragraph each time the speaker changes. Hold up an example of a picture book with dialogue to demonstrate your point.

3. Read the directions for *Separating Speakers* together with students. Explain that they will be making a checkmark next to each new speaker to show where the text should start a new indented paragraph. Point out that each new speaker will have a different color checkmark.

4. Read the passage together with students and ask for volunteers to tell when a new speaker is speaking. Then invite a student to go to the SMART Board and use a SMART pen to place a checkmark in front of the sentence, signaling that it should start a new paragraph. Continue throughout the entire passage.

5. Once the passage has been marked to designate each new speaker, have a student erase the box below the passage to check the corrections. Invite them to count how many times the speaker changed. Have students compare the two versions of the passage, discussing how the correctly punctuated and paragraphed passage aids readers' understanding.

The Inside Story

1. Remind students they have already explored many of the basics of using quotation marks—remembering to use the marks in pairs, distinguishing between exact words and paraphrased statements, remembering to identify the speaker of a quote, and starting a new paragraph for each quote from a new speaker. Explain that in this activity they will explore a skill that is tricky for many writers—correctly using end marks and commas in conjunction with quotation marks.

2. Display *The Inside Story* on the SMART Board. Explain to students that the title suggests an important rule regarding quotation marks: End marks and commas that are part of a direct quote always go *inside* the quotation marks. Read and discuss the rules and examples. Pay special attention to the fact that when a quotation precedes the speech tag (the name of the speaker), a comma is used instead of a period. The other end marks (question marks and exclamation points) do not change.

3. Read the directions with students. Explain that in each of the three scenarios, a student will write a response that applies to what they have learned so far. They will indent for the new speaker, name the new speaker, and correctly place quotation marks and other punctuation.

4. Read the first scenario and have students brainstorm how they might respond. Have a student write the response in the box provided using a SMART pen. Check the response for accuracy of punctuation. If there are mistakes, discuss with students how to fix them. Edit the text accordingly.

5. Repeat step 4 with the remaining scenarios.

Punctuation Power

1. Display *Punctuation Power* on the SMART Board. Explain to students that this page reviews what they have learned about using quotation marks so far.

2. Read the directions for *Punctuation Power* together. Then ask a student volunteer to read the first sentence aloud. Have the volunteer decide which sentence is correctly punctuated and underline it using a SMART pen.

3. After the student has chosen a sentence, have him or her tap the sneaker icon to the right of the sentence. If the sneaker spins around its axis, the student has chosen the correct sentence. If it does not, the class should revisit the pair of sentences to determine which one has the correct punctuation. Use prompts to review relevant rules.

- Are end marks and commas that go with the quote placed inside the quotation marks?

- Do the quotation marks come in pairs?

- When the speaker is named before the quote, is a comma used to separate the speaker from his or her words?

4. If the student volunteer has chosen incorrectly, allow him or her to erase the first underline mark and try again.

5. Repeat the exercise with the remaining sentences.

The Long and Short of It

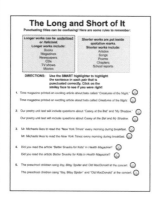

1. Point out that, so far, students have been talking about using quotation marks to set apart a person's words. Explain that another use for quotation marks is to set apart some titles. Activate prior knowledge by questioning students about titles. Challenge them to name different examples of titles. Point out that many kinds of works get titles, from reports students write in school to major Hollywood movies.

2. Display *The Long and Short of It* on the SMART Board. Read the introduction and discuss the rules for punctuating titles. Guide students to understand that longer artistic works, such as books, movies, magazines, and newspapers, are underlined or italicized. (Italics are preferred when using a computer.) Shorter works, or works that are part of a larger work, are set apart with quotation marks. Examples of these shorter works are articles, songs, and poems.

3. Revisit the examples your students generated earlier and decide which type of punctuation each one would receive. Be sure students understand that it is not the length of the title that dictates punctuation; it is the size of the actual artistic work. To clarify, point out that an article is one tiny part of a large magazine. An article title uses quotation marks, while a magazine title gets underlined or italicized.

4. Read the directions and invite students to study the first pair of sentences. Discuss the use of quotation marks and italics in the sentences. Challenge a student (or all students together) to determine which sentence uses quotation marks properly. That student should use the SMART highlighter to highlight the chosen sentence. To access the highlighter, simply go to the SMART pen tool on your toolbar and choose the thick yellow highlighter. This ink will let the original text on the Notebook page show through.

5. Ask a student volunteer to tap on the smiley face icon to check for correctness. If the correct sentence is chosen, the smiley face icon will spin around. If not, the smiley face icon will not move at all. If the incorrect answer is chosen, discuss with students why it was incorrect and have them try again.

Quotation Marks: Your Turn!

1. Print and make copies of *Quotation Marks: Your Turn!* for students. Display the Notebook page on the SMART Board. Explain that students will complete this page on their own to apply what they have learned about quotation marks.

2. Read the directions together with students. Explain that students will add quotation marks where necessary in the passage. Remind them that quotation marks are used to enclose a speaker's exact words as well as the title of a short artistic work.

3. Distribute copies of the worksheet and have students complete the exercise in class or as a homework assignment. Review the exercise individually or as a class to assess student learning.

Apostrophes at Work

Using apostrophes correctly to form possessives and contractions can be tricky, even for adults. This SMART apostrophe unit will help your students meet the challenge!

OBJECTIVES

Students will be able to:

✓ Understand the rules for using apostrophes.

✓ Recognize how apostrophes are used to show possession.

✓ Recognize how apostrophes are used in contractions.

TIME

About 3–4 class periods for Unit 5 (allow 15–20 minutes per lesson)

MEETING THE STANDARDS

This lesson correlates with the following writing standards for grades 3 through 6:

• Students use Standard English conventions in all writing, such as sentence structure, grammar and usage, punctuation, capitalization, and spelling.

• Students review and edit work for spelling, mechanics, clarity, and fluency.

GETTING READY

Before students arrive, have your SMART Board ready to go. Load the Capitalization & Punctuation CD onto your host computer and copy the 5 SMART Apostrophes Notebook file onto your hard drive. Open the local file. The first interactive page, *Amazing Apostrophes*, will appear on your SMART Board. If you wish, use your Screen Shade tool to conceal the page until you are ready to begin.

Amazing Apostrophes

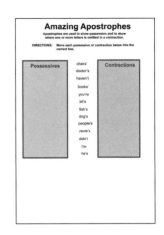

1. Display *Amazing Apostrophes* on the SMART Board. While the words fly onto the Notebook page, take a moment to activate prior knowledge. Ask students to think about where they have seen apostrophes. They will likely respond with specific examples of contractions (*don't*, *I'm*, and so on) and possessives (*Jamal's*, *people's*, and so on). Guide students to notice the two types of examples, pointing out that apostrophes are used to show possession and as a placeholder for missing letters in contractions.

2. Read the directions on the page together with students. Students are asked to identify whether a word is a contraction or a possessive.

3. Have students look at each word in the middle column and determine whether it is a contraction or a possessive. If it is a contraction, invite a student volunteer to drag the word to the purple Contractions box. If the word is a possessive, have the student drag the word into the green Possessives box.

4. As each word is dragged to its correct box, discuss with students how they knew it was a contraction or a possessive. If the word is a contraction, extend learning by asking what two words the contraction stands for.

5. When all the words have been moved into their respective columns, review each column to check for understanding. Invite students to use the SMART pen to add an original example to each box.

All Mine!

1. Display *All Mine!* on the SMART Board. Activate prior knowledge by asking students how they show that something belongs to someone or something (possession). They will likely say that an apostrophe followed by an *s* is used to show possession. Guide students to understand that singular possessives follow this pattern. That is, when one person or thing is the owner, we use the *'s* pattern. Explain that students will practice using this pattern on the page.

2. A clever way to explain the concept of using an apostrophe to show possession is to pretend your arm is an apostrophe by bending it at the elbow to form an apostrophe shape. Then, using a reaching motion, grab an object and say, "It's mine." This is a visual cue to students and a reminder that whenever something belongs to someone or something else, an apostrophe is needed. Students find this little visual demonstration very helpful and will often repeat it when discussing possessives in the future!

3. Read the directions together with students. Draw their attention to the outstretched arm icon.

4. Explain that students will clone the arm and drag it to the word in each phrase that needs an apostrophe. The arm icon has been infinitely cloned, so students can copy it by simply touching and dragging.

5. Read the first phrase together. Discuss what belongs to whom or what. In this phrase, *the dogs bone*, the bone belongs to the dog. Therefore the dog is saying, "It's mine." Invite a volunteer to clone and move the arm icon to the correct spot in the word (between the *g* and the *s*).

6. Repeat step 5 until an apostrophe has been added to each phrase on the Notebook page.

TECH TIP

You will notice that a second arm icon appears at the bottom of the Notebook page. Depending upon the size and location of your SMART Board screen and the height of your students, you may find it easier for students to reach and clone this icon.

Yes, It's an Extra S!

1. Display *Yes, It's an Extra S!* on the SMART Board. Activate prior knowledge by giving students some examples of singular nouns that end in *s* and ask them to make each noun possessive. Guide students to understand that as long as the noun is singular, the rule is still to add *'s*. Point out that plural nouns ending in *s* follow a different rule, which students will explore in the next activity.

2. Read the directions at the top of the page. Explain to students that they will find the word in each sentence that is a possessive noun. After identifying the word, students need to rewrite the word, adding an apostrophe and an *s* to show possession.

3. Invite a volunteer to read sentence 1. In the first box, have the student write the possessive word in the correct form. Afterward, have the student erase the second box (to the right) to check his or her work. The correct answer will appear.

4. Repeat step 3 for the rest of the sentences on the page.

5. After students correct all of the sentences, discuss with them that the rule for possessives requires an apostrophe and then an *s*, even when the word ends in *s* or double *s* (awkward though it may seem at first).

TECH TIP

When students write text on the SMART Board, it is important that they press with a firm hand and not remove the pen from the board in the middle of writing a letter. If students have difficulty, have them practice this skill with the SMART pen on a blank SMART Board page.

Plural Possessives

1. Display *Plural Possessives* on the SMART Board. Activate prior knowledge by asking students to give some examples of plural nouns. If students name only plurals ending in *s*, challenge them to name some unusual plurals. Ask, for example: *What is the plural of child? What do we call more than one goose?*

2. Read the rules at the top of the page aloud, emphasizing that plurals ending in *s* follow one rule, while plural nouns that do not end in *s* follow a different rule.

Forming Plural Possessives

- To form the possessive of a plural noun that ends in *s*, add an apostrophe after the *s*.

- If the plural noun does not end in an *s*, add an apostrophe and an *s*.

---

3. Review the directions, then tackle the first pair of sentences together as a class. Ask students to look at each sentence carefully and to identify which sentence follows the rules for forming plural possessives. Using the smiley face Creative Pen, place one smiley face after that sentence.

4. Tap on the checkmark to see if the class was correct. If students have chosen the correct sentence, the checkmark will spin around. If not, the checkmark will not move.

5. For each remaining pair of sentences, invite a student volunteer to approach the SMART Board and place a smiley face after the sentence he or she believes correctly forms the plural possessive. Then have the student click on the checkmark to check his or her work. If a student chooses incorrectly, review the applicable rule and have him or her try again.

 TECH TIP

When using the Creative Pen to place a single smiley face (or other shape) on the screen, tap the SMART Board with the pen instead of pushing with force. A quick tap puts a single shape on the screen.

Where Did the "O" Go?

1. Display *Where Did the "O" Go?* on the SMART Board. Tell students that with this activity they will begin learning how apostrophes help us form contractions. Elicit some examples of familiar contractions and point out that many contractions are helping verbs combined with the word *not*.

2. Read the introduction to the activity and look at the completed example together. Using the Magic Pen, have a student volunteer circle the letter in WERE NOT that is replaced by the apostrophe. Point out that in most contractions using the word *not*, the *o* is the letter that is replaced by the apostrophe.

3. Invite a volunteer to read the next contraction combination: DID NOT. Have the student use the regular SMART pen to write the correct contraction on the other side of the rainbow. Remind the student to place an apostrophe in the spot where letter(s) are left out. Challenge the student to use the contraction in an original sentence.

4. Repeat step 3 for the remaining word combinations. In each instance, check that the *o* has been omitted and that an apostrophe has been added in its place. Invite each volunteer to orally share a sentence that uses his or her contraction.

5. Direct students' attention to the discussion prompt at the bottom of the page. The prompt highlights two unusual contractions that use the word *not*. In these "rule breakers," letters in addition to *o* are omitted. Have students identify the words that make up each contraction and tell which letters are left out in each case.

6. Tell the students that if they remember the "O" rule (and memorize the two exceptions), they will always know where to place the apostrophe in contractions that use *not*.

 **TECH TIP**

When using these Notebook activities, it's easy to find a spot to record and display notes or ideas. Just scroll down to the bottom of the page and click on Extend Page. Use the extra white space to record your notes. This is a perfect way to record students' sample contraction sentences.

It's a Challenge!

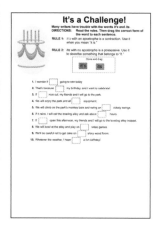

1. Display *It's a Challenge!* on the SMART Board and read the introduction and rules. Point out that *its* and *it's* are homophones—words that sound the same but have completely different meanings. Let students know that many people confuse these two homophones. Emphasize that in this case, the apostrophe is reserved for the contraction *it's*. There is no apostrophe in the possessive pronoun *its*.

2. Have students read the first sentence and discuss which word makes sense in the box. Once you have a consensus, invite a volunteer to drag the correct word to the box. (The words *its* and *it's* have been set up using the SMART infinite cloning tool so that students only need to touch on the word with a finger and drag it across the page. They can do this as many times as needed.)

3. Repeat step 2 for the remaining sentences.

4. Extend the lesson by challenging pairs of students to come up with rhymes or other memory tricks that might help them remember the rules for *its* and *it's*.

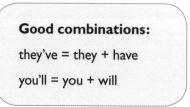

> **Example:**   *It's* with an apostrophe
>
> Is short for the words *it is*, you see!

Contraction Action

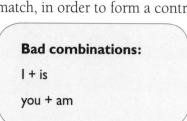

1. Display *Contraction Action* on the SMART Board and tell students they are going to play a game. Divide the class into two equal teams (Team A and Team B). Have each team select an official speaker.

2. Review what students have learned about contractions so far, and explain that in this game students will work with contractions that join pronouns with linking verbs. Share a few examples, and ask students to name the words that make up each example.

> **Good combinations:**
>
> they've = they + have
>
> you'll = you + will

3. Then, share some examples of combinations that do *not* work, such as the ones below. Discuss how the pronoun subject and the linking verb must agree, or match, in order to form a contraction.

> **Bad combinations:**
>
> I + is
>
> you + am

4. Read the game directions with the class. Explain that students will roll the two dice, then use the key to find the words that correspond to the numbers on the dice. The team members will work together to try to make a contraction from the words. If they can make a contraction, that team can record the contraction in its box. If the two words do not combine to form a valid contraction (as in the "bad combinations" shown on the previous page), the team does not record a contraction, and the other team gets to roll.

5. Have a volunteer from Team A touch both dice to roll them. Help the team find the words that correspond to the numbers, then allow a minute or so for the team members to discuss the combination. Ask a team representative whether the team has found a contraction. If so, have the representative approach the SMART Board and write the contraction in the team's box.

6. A contraction must be spelled correctly in order to count. If you or members of the opposing team would like to challenge the validity or spelling of a contraction, use a dictionary to look up the contraction as it is written. A regular (non-children's) dictionary is best for this purpose.

7. Continue, having the two teams alternate until one team has listed ten valid contractions.

TECH TIP

If your kids love using the dice, take advantage of other engaging teaching tools in your Notebook software. Click on the landscape icon on the left side of your SMART Board and select Essentials for Educators. You'll find diagrams, pictures, maps, and ready-to-go Notebook pages on a variety of teaching topics.

EXTENDED LEARNING

Apostrophes: Your Turn!

1. Print and make copies of *Apostrophes: Your Turn!* for students. Display the Notebook page on the SMART Board. Explain that students will complete this page on their own, either in class or for homework, to apply what they have learned about using apostrophes.

2. Read the directions together with students. Explain that the activity is divided into two segments. In Part 1, students will read a series of sentences and decide if each one correctly uses possessives. If the possessive is written correctly, students will rewrite the sentence, correcting the mistake. In Part 2, students will combine words to make contractions and identify the letters that are omitted in each contraction.

3. Distribute copies of the worksheet for students to complete. Review the exercise individually or as a class to assess student learning.